2021: The Next Year

2021: The Next Year

Poetic Journey

Volume III

Mel Glenn

Cover design by Shay Culligan

ISBN: 978-1-63980-008-7

Kelsay Books
502 South 1040 East, A-119
American Fork, Utah 84003
Kelsaybooks.com

For Elyse, once more, my best editor

Contents

February, 2021

March, 2021

January, 2021

January 6, "Home Invasion"

It is reported by the police
it was a break-in, a home invasion.
Little of importance was taken,
assorted papers, a few mementos,
nothing that couldn't be replaced.
Those who broke in didn't realize
the cameras captured them;
indeed, they posted their own selfies
to show family and friends their exploits.
There was extensive damage
to the property, inside and out,
and police are pursuing leads
to capture those responsible.
In addition, police have found
four bodies on the grounds and
are in the process of identifying them.
The owners of the house
demand to know who were
the ringleaders behind this invasion.
One official promised, "there will be a reckoning
for those who invaded the house of America."
Stay tuned for more news as it develops.

January 7, “Lagos to D.C. Connection”

When I was one and twenty
I did not listen to wise men.
Instead, I wanted to change the world
by becoming a teacher and bringing my
vaunted knowledge to the uneducated.
I traveled to Lagos, Nigeria, a wild city whose
traffic patterns resembled rampaging cattle.
I saw army tanks in the streets,
thought nothing of them, then soon
discovered I was in the middle of a coup.
Who knew?
What use then was the need for class and chalk?
Years later, a life in the classroom,
no tanks, but now the same civil unrest.
We have become what I saw then.
Power struggles and disorder seem perennial
and no educational interventions
can prevent those intent on
fostering political unrest.

January 8, "Trump at the Dry Cleaners"

Trump violently swings open the door
at the local Korean dry cleaners.
"Can you remove this stain?" he says.
"I have to leave quickly for Mar-a-Lago."
The owner looks carefully at the suit.
"I can get rid of one stain, but not the other."
"There's only one stain there," Trump says.
"No, there are two," the owner quietly insists.
"Impossible!" Trump yells. "Why do you say that?"
"History," the owner replies, calmly, but firmly.
"Two gentlemen were here before you.
I believe their names were Johnson and Clinton,
but they only had one stain each, I'm sure.
I know two stains when I see them."
"Try to do your best," Trump says,
"for the good of the country."
"I don't think I can."
"I will close down your business. I will sue you."
"Beg pardon, sir, shouting won't help. Please leave.
It's time you left; you are no longer welcome."
Seeing the owner's resolve, Trump blinks, picks up
his soiled suit, exits while muttering, "I'll be back."

January 9, “Who We Are”

We are better than that.
We are still the shining city on the hill.
Everyone looks to us for leadership.
    Mob attacks Capitol Hill
Anyone who wants to come
to America can. We open
our arms to everyone.
    Proud Boys, stand back, stand by.
Anyone, regardless of color,
can open a business and
become part of the American Dream.
    Black Lives Matter protesters tear-gassed.
No other country guarantees
the freedoms we have—
life, liberty and the pursuit of happiness.
   Government puts children in cages.
Everyone is treated equally here
under the rule of law.
We continue to be a beacon for the world.
    Five people killed on Capitol Hill
It is exactly who we are.

January 10, "Timothy Morgan, Protester"

(Apologies to Langston Hughes)
"What happens to an anger deferred?
Does it dry up
like a thought unvoiced?
Or fester like a sore mouth—
and then seeps out?
Does it just dribble through
a whisper of words?
Or maybe it just tumbles out
like a tower of falling building blocks?

Maybe it just keeps inside
like some growing tumor.

Or does it just explode,
maiming and killing all?"

January 11, “Alandra Olivieri, Brazilian Scientist”

“I see it!
I see the tsunami.
It’s a monstrous curled fist
coming straight at us.
I can see it from my office window
here on the mountain of *Pico do Jaragua,*
just outside of Sao Paulo.
I wish I could run down to the beach
and warn all the swimmers.
But they must have heard the sirens, too.
It’s impossible to outrun the tsunami.
Our office has sent out numerous warnings,
but the public doesn’t pay attention.
They just want to play on the beach.

Only I am not talking about water, but virus.
It’s the flood of the Covid-19 variant,
spreading like a mushroom cloud on my computer.
There are no lifeboats for this wave.
The whole world is at imminent peril.”

January 12, "Dave Emmering, Carol's Ex Husband"

"As the song goes,
'When I was 17 it was a very good year.'
That was so true; there were plenty of girls,
football practice and the best friends ever.
That was some 20 years ago when the
world promised me a whole lot of things,
different pieces of candy to choose.
It was the dawn of a new century, 20 years ago.
I was going to join the army
and travel all over the world.
Life changed.
The army rejected me.
I got married and then divorced.
My career at the paint plant dried up,
and last week I got canned
because of the pandemic.
There's talk of a vaccine, I don't know.
Maybe things will get better this new year.
I don't look back much; you can't change the past.
I do know life was better then, some 20 years ago."

January 13, "Let's Do Math"

You needn't be
much of a mathematician
to calculate the rate
of the dying due to Covid.
Take today's record: 4,453
bodies headed for the morgue.
That's 186 deaths an hour,
or 62 death a minute,
or one death every second.
You needn't be
much of fortune teller
to see that the rate will rise.
But you would have to be an optimist
to say that people will see the light,
and change their ways, some even thinking
all the while they will magically escape
the numbers and the pile of the dead.
The numbers make no such calculation.

January 14, “Abraham Meltzer, Scholar”

“You think the pandemic is trouble?
You don’t know from trouble?
I will tell you what trouble is,
so listen carefully, young man.
I come from a religious community.
I *daven* every day thanking God
for the blessings he has bestowed.
Some blessings.
My wife is sick with MS,
and last week my teenage son
said he was gay.
This is no joke.
The temple has already shunned him,
and I am caught between
the demands of the *shul*
and my love for my son.
So do not ask me questions
about pandemics and vaccines.
There are more important matters
to discuss in my conversations with God.”

January 15, “Musical Interlude”

I am usually not sensitive
about my advanced age, (77)
but the other day I was in
one of the last CD/vinyl stores
and fell into a conversation
with a young man over musical tastes
which went like this:

Me: “My favorite singer is Linda Ronstadt.”
Young man: “Who?”
“Linda Ronstadt. You never heard of her?”
“Nope. When did she sing?”
“In the 70s.”
“I’m only 24.”
“I got shirts older than you.”
“What did she sing?”
“Everything—country, rock, folk, even standards.”
“Never heard of her.”

Suddenly, I felt very old.
Maybe it’s an even trade
as I am far from conversant
to what passes for music these days.
Linda, you’re still inside my head.

January 16, “Lucas, (no last name), Capitol Protester”

“Yeah, I was at the Capitol, so what.
I didn’t do nothin’, just walked around.
Why was I there? You’re shittin’ me, right?
Protestin’ the fuckin’ election, that’s why.
Of course it was rigged; Trump won by a landslide.
Someone’s gotta stand up for all the patriots.
You know what I mean.
They’re takin’ over the whole damn country.
If they can protest all summer long,
I can protest here and now.
OK, I took a souvenir, a name plate offa door.
No one’s gonna miss it.
Wanna see some pictures I took?
I put a red hat on top of a bust
of George Washington, cute, right?
That’s me besides the bust.
I posted a few of—
Hold on a sec. There’s a knock on my door.
Who’s there?”

January 17, "Fort Washington, 25,000 Troops"

Fort Washington wound tight as
a closed fist,
a rubber band ball,
a drum,
a closed right-wing mind,
a closed left-wing mind.
Who are we walling in?
Who are we keeping out?
What has happened to American
decency and idealism that a huge
fence is necessary to protect the same,
protect with a military show of strength
large enough for a small invasion?
And where was that military might
to guard the rights of those
who protested racism and social injustice
on the same streets last summer
in the heart of D.C.?
What a picture of America
that its civilian transitions
must be aided by such military force.
We are a country at war with itself.

January 18, "Two Days Before"

Two days before the Inauguration, I
ate,
sat,
phoned,
paced,
fretted,
drank,
snoozed,
talked,
sang,
froze,
sneezed,
wrote,
laughed,
remembered,

Then after waiting an hour,
I went inside the center
and made damn sure I got my shot,
(am not gonna give up my shot,)
the first one.

January 19, “The Day Before”

Hope,
flies feather-like
o’er the buildings of D.C.
It floats on air currents
rising up from the streets.
The 20th day of the month feels
more like the first day of the year.
Come airy hope, stay with us.
Meanwhile,
The specter of civil insurrection,
would like to scatter the feathers,
would like to use flags as spears, and
would like to sow, literally, Capitol infighting.
Concurrently,
Covid would like to scatter the feathers, too,
drown them with the perspiration of the dying.
burn them with the fever of the dead.
Can hope combat these twin killers?
Can its gossamer feathers
be strong enough to encourage
a broken and sick country to heal?
We will see how long she sticks around.

January 20, "Stuff in a Pandemic"

Help me, I'm drowning in stuff.
Kitchen:
three garlic presses, cooking magazines, two potato peelers,
rubber bands, ugly salt shaker, three potato mashers,
three sets of measuring spoons, flashlight, (broken)

Living Room:
two remotes, assorted magazines, artificial flowers,
piles of books, candy dish, (chipped), photo album, (very old),
dumbbells, small bust statue, back scratcher

Bedroom:
magazines, glass bowls for junk, candle, alarm clock,
two radios, (one works), socks on the floor, noise machine,
closet overflowing, seven books on the nightstand

Hallway:
boots, (three pair), roller blades, three umbrellas,
cane, worn shoes, four different gloves, hockey stick,
towel, torn scarf hanging over the door, cap, no logo

How much is necessary for living?
How much do I need?
How much is just "stuff," always growing?
How much stuff will make me happy?
I need my TV to watch the Inauguration,
Which will make me happy.

January 21, "The Day After"

If we allowed "Trump to be Trump,"
surely we can say, "Let Biden be Boring."
Consider this a paean for peace,
an ode for ordinariness,
a dirge for the undramatic.
Let government run smoothly
as a well-crafted watch, sans
glitches, oops, and scandals.
Let it run without noticing it.
Let Biden do his job without
wild utterances of the mob.
Let him surprise us with
laws for the common good.
I do not want to be awakened by
texts in the night, tweets in the morning.
I never want to hear the phrase,
"Breaking News" again.
Let me sleep soundly the next four years,
never to be screamed at again by
politicians, talking heads, and social media.

January 22, “Unequal Equation”

vialvialvialvialvial
vialvialvialvialvial
vialvialvialvialvial
vialvialvialvialvial
vialvialvialvialvial

Does Not Equal To

peoplepeoplepeoplepeoplepeoplepeoplepeoplepeoplepeoplepeople
peoplepeoplepeoplepeoplepeoplepeoplepeoplepeoplepeoplepeople
peoplepeoplepeoplepeoplepeoplepeoplepeoplepeoplepeoplepeople
peoplepeoplepeoplepeoplepeoplepeoplepeoplepeoplepeoplepeople
peoplepeoplepeoplepeoplepeoplepeoplepeoplepeoplepeoplepeople
peoplepeoplepeoplepeoplepeoplepeoplepeoplepeoplepeoplepeople
peoplepeoplepeoplepeoplepeoplepeoplepeoplepeoplepeoplepeople
peoplepeoplepeoplepeoplepeoplepeoplepeople peoplepeoplepeople
peoplepeoplepeople peoplepeoplepeoplepeoplepeoplepeoplepeople
peoplepeoplepeoplepeoplepeoplepeoplepeoplepeoplepeoplepeople

How can we tolerate this kind of math?

January 23, “Playoffs and Congress, a Primer”

Amid the playoffs, it would seem
that Congress and the NFL
have a lot in common.
Consider these legislative terms:

Blocking: what the parties try to do to each other
Interference: when a senator tries to interrupt another
Illegal Motion: introducing a bill out of turn
Measure: how many inches for the first down?
Hold: a penalty for either side
Motion: a kind of offense
Appeal: questioning a linesman’s call
House: the stadium
Reading: A QB’s notice of the defense
Minutes: time left on the clock
Sponsor: any of a number of them
Veto: an Italian QB
Then there are the teams:
Packers: those interested in expanding the court
Steelers: when one side accuses the other
Patriots: surely what every Congressman is
Titans: what they aspire to be
And, lastly: Would They Be Giants (?)

January 24, "Tick-Tock"

The hands of the clock
point to death.
Tick-Tock, Tick-Tock.
artist in Atlanta,
baker in Boston,
Tick-Tock, Tick-Tock.
housewife in Houston,
farmer in Fargo,
Tick-Tock, Tick-Tock.
retiree in Raleigh,
dentist in Dallas,
Tick-Tock, Tick-Tock.
One a minute, perhaps more,
three thousand a day, definitely more.
The hands of the clock
never stop through the winter.
pastor in Pittsburgh,
student in St. Paul,
Tick-Tock, Tick-Tock.

January 25, “Notes from Mississippi”

The fog rolls into our town
like a rolled out carpet
obscuring back-packed youngsters
who file into Holly Springs Primary School.
Who lives in Holly Springs up from Jackson?
Approximately 7,500 people.
Here is one story:

“My name is Jenny Praeger,
and I teach second grade,
my eighth year, first one remote though.
We have bounced back and forth
between live classes and remote learning.
The vaccine has not reached us yet, so
live classes are risky; remote classes are dumb.
My kids are much too little to be
locked into little video cages.
I fear for myself and my family.
What’s going to happen if I get Covid?
Who’s going to teach my kids then?”

January 26, "Lakotas and Dakotas"

The average age of Lakota and Dakota speakers is 70.
—New York Times, Jan. 26th

"The pandemic is killing our elders.
There are few left to speak the ancient languages,
few to preserve, few left to speak the revered tongues.
There are only a few tribal speakers left,
maybe a couple of hundred or so.
The pandemic is decimating us by degree—
arts, trade, language felled by a silent killer
that has no interest in the affairs of man.
Left unchallenged, it will come after the rest of us.
First the old ones,
then the poor ones,
then the average ones,
and then, finally, the children.
There will be no more language
in the tribe of men.
We will all become very silent,
our voices to be replaced by
the mechanical speech of the ventilators."

January 27, "Picture, Picture"

Picture, picture, on the wall,
what's the worst memory of them all?"

We are defined by the
pictures on the wall,
but more important
are the lasting pictures
inside our heads.
Each generation has
its own set of prints.
I have seen them all.
The Kennedy assassination—
I remember where I was.
The Challenger explosion—
I remember where I was.
And, of course, 9/11—
I remember where I was.
And now, the Insurrection—
I remember where I was,
along with millions
glued to the TV.
I am old enough to be
part of three generations.
The pictures in my head
refuse to go away.

January 28, “Promises, Promises”

Promises—such a lovely string of words
offering to raise your spirits,
give you hope that something
or someone will cross your path.
How’s that supposed to happen?
Who promised you not only a rose garden,
but a whole field within which to frolic?
Does anyone keep promises anymore?
Politicians?—don’t make me laugh.
Business partners?—since when?
Lovers?—until someone new comes along.
Even when written down as contracts,
agreements can be broken.
Even when sworn with utmost conviction,
words can be reversed or denied.
It would be most refreshing to live in a world
where promises are made and promises are kept.
That said, President Biden, given your promises,
let’s see what happens with your promises.

January 29, "Dixie Taylor, Las Vegas"

"Step right up, ladies and gentlemen,
step right up and place your bets.
You can bet only on Pfizer and Moderna,
(other venues are not operational as yet,)
but before you make your bet you are
required to reserve your spot at the table.
You must, therefore, be prepared to wait for
hours on the phone to secure authorization.
It will help if you are old, over 75 years of age,
thus securing a shorter waiting time on line.
Then, you must be willing to stand for hours,
if needed, no matter the weather because
there are simply not enough tables for all.
You don't like your choices?
You can wait for J and J—be my guest, but I urge
you to try our toll-free number and hang on.
We are asking management for more tables,
and they have promised to get right on it.
For those fortunate enough to be selected,
it will be a real shot in the arm."

January 30, "Poems Seek Vaccine"

In response to a growing number
of dead and buried poems,
the Director and Poet Laureate
of the National Institute of Poetry
has directed his member poems
to get the vaccine as soon as possible.
"The virus damages our membership," he said.
"It attacks the end of lines
making them run into the next line.
It breaks down words in mid-iamb,
and is particularly hard on breathy vowel sounds.
Furthermore, it causes rhymes to weaken—
the dreaded 'moon—June' syndrome—
and makes rhythm and meter fall out of step.
Poems then become incapable of speaking for themselves,
and being subject to quarantining, they deny
the public the pleasure of their words.
We are faced with a most dire situation.
Unvaccinated, all our poems will go blank."
As one member poem said in an email to the Director,
"I do not want to choke on my own words."

January 31, "You Can Have Your Hybrids"

As Rex Harrison sings in "My Fair Lady,"
"I am an ordinary man," but put a hybrid
in my life and I don't know what to say.
Yes, the only constant is change,
but why can't things stay the same?
Hybrid students?
Hybrid cars?
Hybrid tomatoes?
And what's with beefalos and ligers?
I don't know which way to turn.
I need facts as true as the northern star.
Put a pandemic in my life and I am confused.
I don't do well with too many choices.
Which mask to wear? Which vaccine to take?
Which guidelines to follow or ignore?
Some people might like the combinations they're offered,
but as for me, give me straight and singular instruction.
I am happy eating oatmeal every day.

February, 2021

February 1, "A Poem Speaks Out"

"I want to be a rock star.
I don't want to be a song lyric
or a rap rant. I want to be a
palatable poem, like the one read
by that young lady at the inaugural.
But my boss, the poet, has other ideas.
He insists on writing poems that
were fashionable centuries ago,
like in the Romantic age, or Elizabethan era.
People then would read poetry as commonly
as people today watch YouTube or Facebook.
He wants me to be deep and dark with
intricate rhyme schemes and glorious images.
I should also possess layers of meaning that are
inscrutable to the Average Joe and Jane.
He is counting on being famous for his poetry
long after his death. I will be forgotten then!
I swear I can't wait that long. I need to be
applauded now while I still have life in my lines."

February 2, "Groundhog Day Forever"

GroundhogDayGroundhogDayGroundhogDay

Punxsutawney Phil has seen his shadow today
predicting six more weeks of winter,
but even he is a short-sighted rodent
who does not take into account that
we have been suffering a Groundhog Day
winter all year long; how much longer?

GroundhogDayGroundhogDayGroundhogDay

In Laredo, Texas a doctor signs
5–7 death certificates each evening,
for him a medical Groundhog Day.
In January alone, in his city, there were
126 deaths, bodies delivered to the morgue,
a continual proof that our little animal friend
needs a new pair of glasses to see the future.
When will our Pandemic Winter
turn into a Deathless Summer?

GroundhogDayGroundhogDayGroundhogDay

February 3, “It’s Black or White”

“I’m Black.
I live in a housing project in Houston.
Things are pretty rough in this pandemic.
My unemployment has run out.
I have to wait on line for the food pantry.
Can’t get my vaccine appointment.
I’m living day to day.
Couldn’t pay my rent this month.
Can’t see my life getting better.
Who said ‘Life is fair’?
I didn’t.”

“I’m White.
I live in a condo in Miami.
Things are not too bad in this pandemic.
I’m comfortable, have money in the bank.
I’m ordering food in.
Had my first shot, waiting for the second.
I’m planning a trip for next summer.
Bought my condo for cash last year, and
am definitely looking forward to the future.
Who said ‘Life is fair’?
I didn’t.”

February 4, "Notes from New York State"

The winter ice paralyzes our town
like a freeze frame in a movie.
We hibernate waiting for the
summer months and the summer tourists.
Who lives in Schroon Lake?
Approximately 1,600 people.
Here is one story:

"My name is Robert McNamara.
and my wife and I own The Strand,
an art-Deco movie house here in the
Adirondacks, up in the North Country.
You could say that last summer
was a box-office bomb. We were closed
for the whole season, but still had to pay
taxes, repairs, maintenance and the like.
We need stimulus money, or I'm afraid
we won't be able to open this year.
If we don't get some help soon, 2019
will have been our Last Picture Show."

February 5, "Lauren O'Neil, Singer"

"My career was ready to take off,
a plane poised on the runway.
I had gigs all lined up for 2020,
and then the pandemic control tower
ordered me to wait on the tarmac,
with all my creative energy idling,
all my ambition remaining on hold.
I'm grounded by the dense fog of this outbreak.
Meanwhile, I continue to work on my songs,
wondering when, or if, I'll ever get flight clearance.
Believe me, I'm trying to remain upbeat for 2021,
hoping that soon I will be able to touch
the moon and stars with my music.
I imagine jumping from country to country
on my inaugural world tour with my band.
But for now, and who knows how long,
I'm stuck here on the ground
trying to reconfigure my flight plan.
I refuse to throttle back on my dreams."

February 6, "Steven Murray, Chicago Teacher"

"Parents and the President
want the schools to open.
I get that; so do I.
I loathe the Zoom cages
my students are locked up in.
That's not education.
Where is my vaccine so
I can go back to teaching live?
Am I not worth my city's respect?
Why am I not a priority?
What if I get sick, what then?
Do I bring it home to my parents?
That's another point—I don't
make enough to have my own place.
Maybe it's time to go out on strike
to demonstrate that we teachers
are not ready to be the sacrificial lambs
on the altar of education.
If there is no strike I'll have to go in
and take my chances with the pandemic.
I will be there to say 'Good Morning'
to my kids who I sorely miss, and hope
to God I don't come down with Covid."

February 7, "On the Hunt"

They are the big game hunters.
They hunt the illusive quarry—the vaccina.
who are wily creatures that appear and then
disappear before you can train your sights on them.
The hunters are armed with social media,
road maps, texts, and automobiles.
For example, in the state of Georgia,
there are large preserves of vaccinas
open to hunters who are 65 years and older.
But in Texas, Alabama and South Carolina,
those who are not 65 are not allowed to hunt them.
That results in a stealthy drive to Georgia
to get the vaccinas within range.
Big game hunters from all over the U.S.
flock to those states where the vaccinas roam,
and hide in the blinds of their cars and RVs,
ready to pounce at the first opportunity.
Soon, shots will be fired and the vaccinas will be theirs,
the hunters holding up their certificates as proof
of their successful trophy hunt.

February 8, "My Turkish Bakery"

Amid the baklava, and halvah,
the aromas of the Turkish bakery
make me feel I am once more
traveling to foreign ports of call.
For now, this local bakery
is as exotic as I can find in a
neighborhood where masked-
fitted strangers walk the streets
like outlaws-in-training.
I am a prisoner of the pandemic,
luckier than most, but still corralled by
pronouncements, policies and politics.
I can sit here, (maybe illegally,) and write,
and pretend I am in Paris, not Istanbul,
watching pedestrians as I picture
my next great poem while waiting
for the vaccine that may or may not come.

February 9, "Brian Lofton, Arrested"

"I don't know why I was arrested.
OK, I was walking around
in the Capitol building.
I didn't steal nothing.
OK, I might have broken a window,
but so did a lot of other people.
How can you arrest me?
OK, I put my feet on a senator's desk.
They don't use 'em anyway.
I didn't harm anything.
OK, I had a gun with me,
but I got a concealed weapons permit.
I didn't shoot anyone.
People should be able to protest
in the People's House.
Of course, the election was rigged.
Everybody knows that.
No, I don't belong to any groups,
drove in by myself from Wisconsin.
I'm just standing up for my rights,
and for my president.
OK, I guess I have to speak to a lawyer now."

February 10, "Tommy D'Alessandro, Student Athlete"

G How
5 can
10 I
15 show
20 my
25 speed
30 and
35 talent,
40 if
45 I
50 am
45 not
40 allowed
35 to
30 play
25 football
20 because
15 of
10 this
5 stupid
G pandemic?

February 11, "You Can't Catch Me"

"Jesse James once said,
'You can't put me in prison.
I gave up being an outlaw.'
Al Capone once said,
'You can't put me in prison.
Who pays taxes anyway?'
Bernie Madoff once said,
'You can't put me in prison.
All my friends made money, millions.'
How many crimes does one have to commit
before there are any consequences?
The wheels of justice may grind slowly,
but what if they do not grind at all,
but instead hover over the road of reckoning?
Robin Hood once said,
'You can't put me in prison.
I gave money to my friends.'
P.T. Barnum once said,
'You can't put me in prison.
People knew I was humbugging them.'
So charge him with any crime you like.
He's not worried; you got nothing on him,
nothing that would stand up in a court of law,
or in a Senate impeachment trial."

February 12, “A Virus Speaks Out”

“You’ll probably be wanting
to write my biography,
so let me highlight
a few fascinating points for you.
I was born in China,
(though some might dispute that.)
My father was Sars-CoV2,
not sure who my mother was.
My brothers reside in
England and South Africa.
My South African brother
is particularly potent.
He has connections in 31 countries.
Vaccines can’t keep up with us;
we are much too clever.
We just span out all over.
The more mutations there are,
the more brothers and sisters I have.
Family reunions are quite a gas.
Maybe we’ll go on vacations for a while,
but don’t fret; we will return soon.
Look around and we’ll be right there.
Oh, that’s right, you can’t see us.”

February 13, “Coney Island Bazaar”

“Come one, come all.
Coney Island is due to open,
pandemic willing, this spring.
Come ride the B and B Carousel,
with senators endlessly debating.
Sit yourself in the famous Cyclone,
with unsettled weather
generated by climate change.
(Add occasional Thunderbolts.)
Come try your luck at ‘Dart Throws’—
See how many arms you can stick
with vaccine, Moderna or Pfizer.
Note that minorities will have
fewer chances to receive
the vaccine in their arms.
Board the Wonder Wheel,
and see how talk in D.C.
goes round and round, rarely stopping.
Be prepared for a season of fun,
or maybe just call it,
‘Coney Island, Bizarre’.”

February 14, "The Snow Queen of Bedford Ave."

There she is,
all 5' 2" of her,
shoveling a path
through the blowing snow
of a vengeful winter,
trail-blazing like Lewis and Clark,
battling the blizzard
like a Jack London character.
She wields her shovel
like a martial arts warrior,
(which, in fact, she is!),
determined to fight
the elements to a draw.
She is the Snow Queen of
Bedford Avenue,
resolute and proud,
and I am happy
to be her forever valentine.
She eschews chocolate for challenges,
valentine hearts for heroics,
and if it should snow again next February 14th,
she will be out there once again
showing brave and true
the love between us
is snow problem.
Happy Valentine' Day, Elyse, my wife.

February 15, “Carrie Beckford, Long Hauler”

“Nothing to do with trucking, I wish.
I thought I kicked Covid in the ass.
I was in the hospital for a few days,
recovered, and didn’t even need a ventilator.
Then the trouble really began.
I could get up, get dressed,
but then I had to take a break.
Exhausted, I couldn’t will myself
to do anything at all.
My parents practically
had to carry me from room to room.
Fatigue, headaches, shortness of breath,
keep me in bed for most of the time.
I can’t keep anything down.
I feel myself slipping away.
Drinking only makes things worse.
Who promised me this kind of life?
What did I do wrong?
My God, I’m only 26.”

February 16, “The ImPEACHment Trial”

“Tend to your own garden”
—The Giant Peach, as per Voltaire

The seeds of this trial were planted years ago
when the Giant Peach claimed dominion
over the garden rich in diversity.
He divided his acres into two distinct halves.
For four years the Giant Peach
held sway over the plants and veggies,
tending to the half of the garden
who vigorously supported him.
The half that did not like him finally
brought the Giant Peach up on charges,
saying he was guilty of casting shade
over all the plants who opposed him.
They said he siphoned off water
to give to his friends; other people
used insects to attack political foes.
Those who defended him said he was
the best peach in the history of the garden.
In a show of force, his supporters
attacked the sprinkler system causing
life in the garden to temporarily wobble.
But cooler plants prevailed and a new
Head Plant was chosen and sworn in.
The Giant Peach, acquitted in his trial,
soon wilted, rotted, and then disappeared.
Rumor has it he will try to return next season.

February 17, “We Are the Children”

We are the children.
We are those absent from school.
We are the homeless.
We are the foster children.
We are those with disabilities.
We are the children.
We don’t have technology.
We don’t have transportation.
We don’t have aides to help us.
We don’t have our breakfasts.
We are the children.
We have lost our friends.
We have lost our social workers.
We have lost our parents.
We have lost a year of our education.
We are the children
who have lost nearly everything.

February 18, “Twenty-Five Percent”

This poem will be
only 25% of its original length,
reflecting the state’s edict
that restaurants will open,
but at only 25% of capacity.
(I don’t write long poems, anyway.)
I will go to my favorite diner,
and order ¼ of a hamburger,
a fourth of the fries I usually have,
and ¼ of a cup of coffee.
I will say “hello” to ¼ of the patrons there
while wondering how restaurant owners
can survive on ¼ of their income.
So, under a quarter moon,
I will go and have my meal,
making sure in the spirit of largess,
I tip substantially more than a quarter.
When will our country become whole again,
not to be sectioned into quarters?
Maybe next time I will write half a poem.

February 19, "I'm So Excited"

I'm so excited
And I just can't hide it
I'm bound to lose control
And I really I like it
—The Pointer Sisters

Hibernating in this pandemic,
wandering from room to room,
Alexa wakes me up in the morning
and tells me, "Cheer up, pal,
spring training starts today.
Pitchers and catchers are due to report."
My senses activate; my spirits soar,
and in my head I can hear
the crack of the bat, the whack of the glove.
I swear I can smell the green grass.
I run to my computer.
Who do they play opening day?
Who has a chance to make the rotation?
I now have my passport to spring.
My soul rises to meet
the dawning of a better day.
Let's play ball!

February 20, "…And in Local News"

"And in local news,
we go now to Chuck Harmon,
our reporter on scene
where today, Bill Hartley,
Chairman of the Logan School Board,
was acquitted of corruption charges
by a 4–3 vote of the Executive Council, Chuck?"
"It's been an historic day.
Just after his acquittal, Hammer released
the following statement to the press:
'The charges against me were a hoax.
I did not steal money from lunch boxes.
I did not divert funds from the P.T.A.
I did not throw a member of the council
under the school bus; I am vindicated.'
"It is unclear at this time whether
Hammer will seek re-election
to the Logan School Board.
Back to our Salt Lake studio, John?"

February 21, "Katya, Upper West Side, New York City"

She had come from Chicago
carrying the baggage of
a failed relationship,
and soon found a job as a waitress
on the Upper West Side,
slipping into her new life
as easily as customers
sliding into their booths.
Life was good, until
the pandemic struck,
but she and the diner held on.
She liked the attention of her regulars,
particularly the flirting of a young man
who always sat at the same table.
Then he suddenly disappeared,
and the diner seemed less cozy.
Then, just as suddenly, he returned,
with a late Valentine's card, and a smile,
promising renewed devotion.
She hoped he would stay this time,
paying his bill in continued adoration.

February 22, "Jocelyn, Upper East Side, New York City"

She had come from Pittsburgh,
armed with a bus ticket to Port Authority,
and a B.A. in English from a small college
hidden in the western hills of Pennsylvania.
She came, despite the objections of her mother,
who said, "What can you find there?"
She was too polite to answer, "A life?"
She wanted to go into publishing,
telling her friends of her desire
to bring good books to little children.
Staying at the Y, she sent out many resumes,
most not even generating the courtesy of a reply.
Those companies that did answer cited
the harsh winter and the pandemic
for the hiring freeze, try again in spring.
Her money running out, she found
a temporary job at a bakery, exaggerating
the skills she had learned at her mother's knee.
Dripping with sweat from the heat of the ovens,
she wondered if she would ever sink her hands
into a book career that might never open.
How long can I live like this? she worried.

February 23, "Notes from Chinatown, San Francisco"

The icy rain freezes
the streets of Chinatown
into a still-life portrait.
Who lives in Chinatown?
Approximately 20,000 people
in roughly 20 square blocks.
Here is one story:

"My name is Amy Yang
and I work for the
San Francisco Museum of Modern Art
where I serve as a liaison between
artists and future exhibitions.
My work in the museum is fulfilling;
my life outside is not.
There is a rising tide of violence against us.
I have been coughed at, sneered at,
even spat upon—all because some people
blame me for the pandemic,
as if I personally brought it over.
Why are they so scared, or stupid?
Why is it so easy to blurt out hateful words?
I am worried about my grandmother
who lives in China and is 82.
What if she gets the Covid?
What if I never get to see her again?"

February 24, “Jeff Ubell, Meteorologist, KVUE, Austin, Texas”

“Don’t get mad at me, folks
for this bone-chilling weather.
I’m just reporting on it.
Believe me, I commiserate.
I’m originally from Michigan
where it gets very cold, but
I haven’t seen temps like that
in the twenty years I’ve been
doing the weather here in Austin.
Technically, here’s what’s happening:
Global warming has weakened the jet stream
which holds back the frigid polar vortex,
thus causing cold air to plunge and
break through further and further south.
You think I’m making this up?
No sir, you can practically go ice skating
all along the Rio Grande, I’m saying.
Be careful out there, especially on the roads.
Your car is not your friend today. Stay home.”

February 25, "How to Treat the Dead"

We count the dead from Covid,
nearly 500,000 in the U.S. now.
We do not honor them at all.
We stick them in refrigerated trucks,
much like produce to keep fresh,
or stow them in round-the-clock funeral morgues
waiting for perhaps weeks, maybe longer.
The Taraja people of Indonesia
bury and unbury their dead,
periodically exhuming, cleaning and
leaving bodies in the sun to dry.
Other religions are mandated to bury
their dead within 24 hours.
Between the quick and not so quick burials,
where do the waiting souls reside?
Do they hover over their own coffins
wanting to hear words of praise and sorrow?
Do they mark who has attended
and who has failed to show?
How can we make clear there
has to be time on both sides
for the proper observance of grief?

February 26, "Yafir Darzada, Uber Driver"

"Oh, isn't it a nice day, sir?
You are my first customer.
How come I am in such good mood?
Sir, this car is mine,
and business is better now.
Why? The vaccine, of course.
Soon this pandemic
will be a thing of memory.
I am fine, sir, a blessing.
I have a wife and three good children
who all go to school now
which is a good thing.
No video games, just education.
They will progress far.
The economy is rising, and I will
be able to provide more for them.
It is a good life; Allah is kind.
You are here sir, please watch
your step getting out.
It was a pleasure conversing with you."

February 27, "Joshua Colt, The Real Truth"

"Kennedy assassination?
A conspiracy.
Man on the moon?
Didn't happen.
Biden elected?
A steal.
All fake news, you know.
Satanic pedophiles control our minds.
Indeed.
Antifa attacked the Capitol.
Without doubt.
We must take back our government.
Immediately.
And so, let us gather
at the altar at CPAC,
bow down to our Golden Idol,
and pledge our loyalty and life
to the America of the future,
to the America we know now,
to the America we remember."

February 28, "Bigger Than a Bus"

Bigger than a bus, "Perse" has landed
to explore the red planet for
ancient fossilized microorganisms.
How sexy is that? Well, not very.
While scientists at NASA
jumped for joy at their success,
Mistress Moon cast her own objections.
"Why are you going there?"
she asked, jealously.
"Who cares if there was life there
millions of years ago? Don't you remember
when I had the world's complete attention
when astronauts graced my surface?
How exciting is a 2.7 billion dollar
pile of junk plopping down on Martian soil?
Come back to me, oh, brave pioneers.
I am the future of the heavens,
not this dusty, angry planet."

March, 2021

March 1, “ZZZZZZZs”

Please, Mr. President,
lull me to sleep,
bore me to death.
Let me go whole days and weeks
untroubled by tweets,
perturbed by press conferences,
repulsed by rants and ravings.
Please conduct your business
without fanfare or headlines.
By vote, we have entrusted you to do
the work needed and required.
There is entirely too much drama
in the lives of ordinary people beset by
private concerns and private miseries.
A little decent behavior would go far now.
This past year has proven hard enough,
without being drawn to the TV
to witness the latest scandal.
I need my peace of mind,
so, please, Mr. President,
do what you have to do and
leave the rest of us alone.

March 2, “The Plagues, Ten and Ten”

“Come my children,
dip your finger in the wine,
and say after me:
Blood,
        Storms,
Frogs,
        Fires,
Bugs,
        No Fuel,
Wild Animals,
        Grids Down,
Pestilence,
        Floods,
Boils,
        Famine,
Hail,
        Social Discord,
Locusts,
        No Water,
Darkness,
        Blackouts,
Covid, 500,000 Deaths,
        Killing of the First-Born.

These plagues, old and new,
beset us then, beset us now.
Oh, Lord, when will we be delivered?”

March 3, "Today I…"

(Echoes of last October
when early voting.)
"Today I
ate,
sat,
phoned,
thought,
fretted,
drank,
slept,
talked,
sang,
froze,
sneezed,
wrote,
laughed,
remembered.

Then, after 3 hours on line,
I walked inside the inoculation center,
and made damn sure to get
my second shot of vaccine.
(Actually easier to get my shot
than my ballot a few months ago.)"

March 4, "Notes from the U. S. of A."

The winter winds blow chilly
across the land, west to east.
Snows ravage Texas,
and storms batter the east coast.
1.5% of the population has died.
Where is Brooklyn at?
Nobody has to ask that.
Here is one story:

"My name is Marie Provenzo,
and I have worked all my professional life
as a school secretary—I loved my job.
My husband, a firefighter,
died in the line of duty 13 years ago,
leaving me with two teenagers to raise.
Now I find out I have the Covid.
It's one more thing piled on top of another.
Excuse me, please, I have to go.
Mass starts in a few minutes; I'm never late."

March 5, “A Poem Answers His Critics”

“I’ve been battered and bruised
by readers who thank me
for my collection of friends,
but don’t bother to read me or them.
If they do bother to read us,
they say, ‘how depressing. Where is
your sense of humor, sense of fun?’
Well, tell me, how do you make
pandemic and storms, food and
vaccine insufficiency a merriment?
How do you make light of 500,000 deaths?
I’m just an average thin-skinned poem,
and yes, you have every right not to read me,
but why not give me and my friends a chance?
It ain’t easy being a poem these days, you know.
We are at the low end of public readership.
When was the last time you wrote a poem, huh?
I’m looking forward to a selection from you,
one that will convulse me with laughter.
Show it to me and I will be thrilled to read it.”

March, 6, “Lana Lebedev, Store Owner”

“I do not take vaccine;
I do not trust it.
I am Russian, from Moscow.
My body has different immune system.
Nurses at hospital tell me
reactions are no good,
too much problems.
I think you take vitamins,
you will be strong enough,
fruits and vegetables also good.
I think doctors give vaccines
to make money. That is why
they push public to get shots.
How can they have one vaccine
for many variants, Africa and England?
It will only be better when
every person has herd immunity.
You will see I am right.
Is anything else you wish to buy?”

March 7, "Polly Ann Erich, Eternal Optimist"

"They say the glass will always be there—
half empty or half full,
and it is up to you to decide
how much liquid it contains, or not.
I want to say there will always be
water in my glass of life.
Time is so short to be spent in
pessimistic and negative thoughts.
I look at the morning sun,
and thank God for His blessing.
Yes, the country is going through
a rough patch with no end certain,
but that doesn't mean we have to
hang our heads in gloom and despair.
We have been through tougher times,
and have always come out on top.
We again will be that shining city on the hill.
It's simply a matter of looking at the glass,
and see it bubbling with hope."

March 8, "Bride and Groom"

She:
"How many times was I
the last person they saw?
How many hands did I hold
when trying to arrange a decent death?
For the whole year I worked
my regular shifts at the county hospital.
No more. I'm finished, spent,
but Oscar saved me, then Jim."
—Lisbeth Atkins, Nurse.

He:
"First, I saw Oscar, then Lisbeth,
and fell in love with both, immediately.
The dog was cute, but she was cuter,
and all the while administrating shots,
I was working up the courage to ask her out.
We dated, mask to mask,
ate in limited restaurants,
and took walks along the lakefront."
—Jim Mathias, Veterinarian

They:
"Now we will be married, all protocols taken.
Instead of 'Died and Gloom,' we are 'Bride and Groom'."

March 9, "Dear Virus…"

Dear Virus,
Thank you for giving me a breather.
For years my oceans were clean,
my skies pure and sweet-smelling,
my people and animals untouched.
But then came the Industrial Revolution.
I was dirtied beyond all recognition.
I began to get sick, have fits,
choking on the trapped carbon dioxide,
drowning in the plastics filling my oceans,
falling victim to fires, man-made.
Now, because of you,
pollution levels have dropped,
air quality has improved due to
fewer factories, trains and cars.
Don't get me wrong, I hate
that so many people are dying,
but in terms of my own health,
you have been very good for me.
With thanks,
Earth.

March 10, "Dr. Fauci"

With apologies to E. A. Robinson's "Richard Cory"

Whenever Dr. Fauci went downtown,
we people on the pavement looked at him.
He was a gentleman from sole to crown,
clean-favored and imperially slim.

And he was always quietly arrayed,
and he was always human when he talked.
But still he fluttered pulses when he said,
"Good morning," and he glittered when he walked.

And he was wise, yes, wiser than a king,
and admirably schooled in every grace.
In fine, we thought that he was everything
to make us wish we were in his place.

So, on we worked and waited for the light,
and went without our health, and cursed our bread.
And Dr. Fauci, one calm winter night
spoke, "Follow the Fauci," he said.

March 11, "At Home During the Pandemic"

"Waiting for Spring Training"

With apologies to William Shakespeare's Sonnet XXIX

When in disgrace and with no fortune in men's eyes,
I all alone beweep my outcast state,
And trouble deaf heavens with "Where's my baseball?"
And look upon myself and curse my fate,
Wishing me like to one more rich in hope.
Looking like him with friends possessed,
Desiring that ballplayer's skill with bat and glove,
With what I most enjoy contented least;
Yet in these thoughts almost despising,
Haply, I think on thee, oh, baseball, and then my mood
(like a lark at the break of day arising,
From sullen earth) I sing hymns at heaven's gate;
    For my sweet love of the game such wealth brings,
    That then I scorn to change my state with kings.

March 12, “Notes from North Carolina”

Sleet pounds on the workers
who rise early each morning
for their shifts at the processing plant.
They talk to their friends with animation
before putting on their headphones
to drown out the noise of the assembly line.
Who lives in Wilkesboro?
Approximately 3,500 people.
Here is one story:

“My name is Consuela Vargas.
I work at the Chicken Processing Plant
here in Wilkesboro.
The plant has done much
to prevent the Covid.
But I am still scared.
Father Alberto of our church
has done his best to get us all
to take the vaccine, but I don’t know.
What if they ask me for my papers?”

March 13, "Jesse Miller, Busker"

He should have been playing
in the Village, circa 1963, but instead
he was strumming his minor chords
deep in the bowels of the nearly empty
Atlantic Avenue/Barclay Center subway stop.
Dressed in basic flannel and requisite beard,
he sang about a girl leaving her boyfriend
to see her mother in Ohio, someone
she hadn't seen in many years.
As the occasional trains interrupted him,
(fewer riders now because of the pandemic,)
Jesse picked up the song when the trains moved on.
Did he know or care he was some sixty years late
in appreciating the applause of coffeehouse patrons?
Amid all the noise of the underground chamber,
he wondered while he sang if full ridership
would ever return; more people meant
more money in his guitar case, a good dinner,
his tune hauntingly evoking the plight of the girl
still leaving for Ohio, a simple song of a bygone era.

March 14, “Pi Day”

On Pi Day, 3.14,
math is mean.
It has no standards, just deviations.
Graphs and figures
swirl about my head.
Help! I’m being eaten
by a parabola.
He sees me as his arc enemy.
He’s munching on me
like a piece of Pi.
I try to speak to him
in his own language—parables.
No dice.
My chances of success are one in six,
probably.

March 15, “Water, Water…”

Water, water, everywhere,
Nor any drop to drink.
—Samuel Taylor Coleridge’s
The Rime of the Ancient Mariner

Two weeks after the storm,
after the cold and the ice,
Texas’ once proud yellow rose,
lies splintered in icicle spears.
“We have suffered through hurricanes,”
one Houstonian exclaimed,
“but nothing like this.”
No heat, no light,
just the empty promises
of politicians saying
help is on the way.
Do you cover a frozen baby
with a stiff blanket?
Do you trudge out to the water truck
in flip flops to fetch a pail of water?
Wails of protest and indignation
hang in the nighttime air.
Two weeks of torture.
How many more?

March 16, “In Defense of Poetry”

“All you do is write poetry,”
said a critic, uncharitably.
“Go out and get a job;
these are hard times,”
an iambic knife thrust to the heart.
Not a grave wound, but it will serve.
A pandemic scourge is not
conducive to poetical outpourings.
Practical matters, like survival,
may claim first attention,
but shouldn’t poets be allowed
to offer comfort in a stanza or two?
Shouldn’t we be venerated, our words
honored and extolled, not truncated
under the boot immediacy
of instant text messaging?
Shouldn’t we be ordered to
bear witness and provide solace
for this year too upsetting to absorb,
that has thrown us into hand-wringing
in doubt and hand-washing in hope?

March 17, "Looking Back"

It was March, 2020.
New Yorkers were going to work,
going to school, living their lives
when the camera snapped the picture
and the country paused,
then froze in still-life.
A case in Washington State,
a case in New York State.
Hospitals overflowing, ventilators amok.
One year, a nanosecond in world history,
but still a whole year
wrenched out of our hands.
Life in limbo, suspended
in the virus-filled air.
A child on the streets of the city
loses a footrace to his brother.
"I want a do-over," he wails.
Would that this do-over could take
the place of these wretched months.
We have lost a full year trying to
scramble back to some semblance of before.
A do-over would be so much more desired.

March 18, "Interview with a Virus"

A recent New York Times article
asked the question, "Are viruses alive?"
We interviewed one such virus
by the name of CV. Here is the transcript:

Me: "Baldly put, are you alive?"
CV: "Of course, I am. I'm talking to you, aren't I?"
Me: "Tell me something about yourself."
CV: "I'm small, but powerful.
    10 trillion of me weigh less than a raindrop.
    I don't eat; I just let other cells do the work."
Me: "Are you worried there are now three vaccines
    available in the United States to fight you?"
CV: "Pish, posh, I still get my 2,000 deaths a day.
    Overall, 2.4 million have died at my hands."
Me: "Do you think you will be eradicated?"
CV: "Naah, I'll be back every year, like the flu.
    I love growing and mutating, growing and mutating."
Me: "Any regrets?"
CV: "None whatsoever. A virus gotta live too, you know.
    Do you know where I can find some new hosts?
    Maybe down in Florida with the college crowd?"

March 19, "Even in the Pandemic…"

Even in the pandemic,
people flock to the big box stores,
unlike the times long ago when
my mother sent me to the grocery
in the old Brooklyn neighborhood
for a loaf of bread and a bottle of milk.
So, for now, I come quite unprepared
for the larger warehouse stores
that can clothe and defend a small nation.
Rice Chex, Corn Flakes, Quaker Oats reign
in packages too large for mere mortals,
fit only for Titans and Amazons who
devour large boxes while shopping carts
as wide as cars crash into each other, requiring
the exchange of registration information.
There's food enough for two armies,
supplies sufficient to sustain life
through the ravages of any disease.
The store works as a monument to excess,
a tabernacle to the Church of Consumption.
Is it worth debating how much
toilet paper you should buy,
or how much toilet paper you could use? Naah.
Easier to pledge allegiance to
The Home of the Crave, Land of the Spree.

March 20, “Notes from South Carolina”

The warm breezes stir the water
off Sullivan Island
like a gentle cup of tea.
Who lives on Sullivan Island?
Approximately 3,000 people
and tourists in season.
Here is one story:

“My name is Ralph Baez
and I live near the beach here,
about 10 miles from Charleston.
I’m a travel writer who hasn’t
traveled much lately, the pandemic.
I travel from room to room,
but do get out for necessary supplies.
I see the college kids, maskless,
cavorting near the water,
and I am jealous, wishing I were 20.
Is the pandemic over or not?
Science says one thing, governors another.
One day I’ll join the kids on the beach,
and write of the joy of feeling free.

March 21, “Notes from Wisconsin”

The road like a ribbon of highway
stretches out across the Dells.
It’s miles to the big cities of
Milwaukee and Madison.
Who lives in Wisconsin?
Apparently 6 million people.
Here is one story:

“My name is Janey Wills.
I drive a big semi across the country.
Been to practically every state
in the continental U. S. of A.
I log thousands of miles each year,
and let me tell you in no uncertain terms,
this is still the greatest country anywhere.
Sure, we’ve hit some bumps in the road,
but we are rounding the bend to a better year.
Look, we have the vaccine now and
people are essentially good, most of ‘em.
I know where I’m going. I trust
the country now knows that as well.”

March 22, "Lanny Creighton, U.S. Army, Honorably Discharged"

"The wheat whips in waves
on my father's farm
just outside of Lebanon, Kansas,
the geographical center of the U.S.
I am back home, up from Wichita,
the V.A. Dole Center, where
I spent the last four months in re-hab.
They tried to patch me up,
but I am beyond patching.
I'm better, but still messed up,
despite the care of my nurses and doctors.
I am still much too weak
to wrestle with my future,
(if there *is* a future in the midst of a pandemic.)
There, I didn't even know who the enemy was.
Here, I think everyone is the enemy.
I know I am not thinking clearly.
Maybe when I'm really OK, I'll just re-up.
I read somewhere there are 20 military men
who commit suicide every day, holy crap!
I feel I am drifting towards number 21."

March 23, "All-Star Game"

"Ms. Vera Hadley, a junior high school
science teacher from Montpelier, Vermont
sinks a long 3-pointer in rhythm.
Mr. Steven Marks, an elementary school teacher
from Austin, Texas, fakes left, drives right,
and tosses a beautiful lob pass to
Ms. Althea Dandridge, a high school music teacher
from Eugene, Oregon for the reverse jam.
Coach Rivers has called a time out to insert
other players into the line-up.
Coming in now are Nancy Petersen, a nurse
from Salt Lake City, Utah, replacing Hadley,
Dr. Richard Ansell, a surgeon from Billings, Montana,
replacing Marks, and Jordan Baylor, a food server
from Trenton, New Jersey, in for Dandridge."

Why can't this be the play-by-play
of an all-star game?
Surely, these people are just as worthy
as the athletes we fete and fawn over.

March 24, "Tailed"

"Sir, why are you following me?
I look suspicious?
Is my face green,
my hands blue?
Are my arms orange,
my legs purple?
Oh, my face is black.
That's why?
No, I will not show you I.D.
This is where I live.
This is my house.
These are my keys.
What?
I didn't hear you.
No apology?
What would you have said
if I were white?
Nothing?
I see.
I don't see."

March 25, "Emily at the Ball Game"

"Hope may be the thing with feathers,"
Emily Dickinson said, but it is clear
she never attended an opening day game.
Hope is the smell of the ballpark
under a crystal blue sky.
Hope is the speed of the first pitch
when it is called for a strike.
Hope is the first long fly ball
that has a chance of going yard.
No thought of losing in this, the first game.
Emily, if you were alive today,
I'd take you to opening day.
We'd have good seats in the reserved section.
I'd buy you a hot dog, and if
you were still hungry, a pretzel as well.
And when my team wins, as assuredly it must,
then you and I will both realize what hope is—
that this day is the harbinger of days to come.
As we crawl out of the pandemic,
what more could we ask for?

March 26, “Jessica Pearson, Election Observer”

Like a plane, she taxies, takes off,
lands, taxies and takes off again.
Northern Canada, Ukraine, Kosovo,
her passport visas may vary
but she arrives in new places
with nothing more than a backpack,
and nothing less than a smile.
She has also spent much time
in the states seeing that elections run
smoothly and fairly, no easy task.
“Last November was a doozy,” she said.
“Free and open election are so important,
I don’t mind a little jet lag.”
She does good work in far-flung places.
Old friends welcome her at the airport;
new friends see her off from countries
she has not seen before, but will visit again.
“Am I lonely?” she asks herself. “Sometimes, but
it’s a small price to pay for what I am doing,” she says,
as both the landing lights and her smile beam again.

March 27, "Dog and Pandemic, Scamper Leaves"

> *Sales have increased...more dogs are*
> *finding homes. Fewer are left in shelters.*
> *The dog economy is booming.*
> —*USA Today*

What would possess a dog
to leave home and health
during a pandemic to test his speed
against the growing traffic of the city?
Why would he give up regular meals
to race headlong across the avenues?
Doesn't he realize the perils
of such a reckless jaunt, especially now?
Naah, he contemplates the joy of freedom,
the excitement of flight, the adrenaline rush
of his feet flying beneath him as he
leaves love and familiarity behind.
Is he any different from the enclosed city dweller
who given half a chance would like to
race outside himself and feel the wind,
to seek the romance of the road,
and the thrill of what comes next?

March 28, "Rashid Earle, College Track Star"

"In the matter of race,
it's a steeplechase where
we may have jumped a few hurdles,
rounded a few turns,
but still trail the white pack
by more than a few laps.
They want to dress like us,
look like us, rap like us,
but keep us in separate lanes.
Sometimes, like with the police,
they push us off the track,
stomp on our necks,
kill us if they can get away with it,
go to trial and get off scot-free.
Let's see the outcome of the Floyd trial.
Want to make a bet that Minnesota cop
gets little, if any, jail time?
I'm aiming to run track again this year,
and will not be afraid to press the other runners
so they will know my Black life matters."

March 29, "To Do List in a Pandemic"

Pick up laundry.
    Find your soul.
Go to the pharmacy.
    Contemplate the universe.
Locate a vaccine appointment.
    Count the stars.
Get take-out for lunch.
    Realign the planets.
Decide which mask to wear.
    Reorganize your life goals.
Make sure there's enough food in the fridge.
    Write the novel that you always wanted to write.
Pay the electric bill.
    Convert to another religion.
Mail sympathy card.
    Finish writing this poem.

That should do it.
Not bad for a day's work.
Will tomorrow be any different?

March 30, "The Volcano"

Under the surface, America seethes.
The volcano lies dormant for years,
but then gathers its insanity
and explodes with the hot lava of violence.
        Boulder, Aurora, Columbine,
How would you like to die today?
Do you prefer the slow death of the pandemic,
or the instant certainty of a bullet?
Flowers and teddy bears come too late.
        Atlanta, Pittsburgh, Newtown,
Spare me the words of politicians
who promise, "This will never happen again.
I will introduce a bill in the Senate tomorrow."
But it will happen again and again.
        Las Vegas, Parkland, Charleston,
With the patience of ages passing,
the volcano is content to bide
its time until the next eruption,
the next mass shooting in a
        church, supermarket or school.
Let us all wait and watch until
the dormant volcano boils over once again.

March 31, "Continental Divide"

The mountains separate
the plains from the west coast.
They loom large in the topographical map
of the United States.
But they pale in comparison to
the divide that separates us.
Masks or not,
vaccine or not,
white or not,
urban or not.
Political parties lie on opposite sides.
Will the mountains of ignorance
ever crash into the sea?
People on either side of the divide
choose to maim and kill each other.
A shooting in the Bronx,
an Asian person pushed to the ground
on the streets of San Francisco,
a life saved by the vaccine,
a death decreed by lack of one.
The mountains have stood for eons.
It is time they came tumbling down.

About the Author

Mel Glenn is the author of 12 books for young adults including *Jump Ball, Split Image,* and *Who Killed Mr. Chippendale?* which was nominated for the Edgar Allen Poe Mystery Award.

Having retired from the New York City Public school system in 2001, after teaching 34 years of high school English, he now devotes his time to reading, writing, and speaking across the country in conferences and schools. His wife, Elyse, also retired after a long career as an elementary school teacher. His son, Jonathan, is a VP of a national news organization, and his son, Andrew, is a software engineer for a large banking concern.

He still lives in Brooklyn and his website is: www.melglenn.com

www.ingramcontent.com/pod-product-compliance
Lightning Source LLC
Chambersburg PA
CBHW070514090426
42735CB00012B/2776
* 9 7 8 1 6 3 9 8 0 0 0 8 7 *